you are not ugly

you are not ugly

saniya kaushal

ISBN: 978-1-7772299-1-7 (paperback)
ISBN: 978-1-7772299-2-4 (ebook)

Illustrations and cover design by Saniya Kaushal
First printing edition 2020.

Published by Saniya Kaushal
www.saniyakaushal.com

for anyone who has ever
questioned their worth

my family

i am grateful

to have been showered

with unconditional love

since the day i left the womb

thank you to the three who have built me

table of contents

feel...

you are not ugly

reckless words being spit out in seconds

she mocks his thin arms

the same ones he used

to push his drunk father

off of his mother

last night

you are not ugly

scratched

chipped

cracked

shattered

brave and broken

he glued the pieces back together

just for another person to come along

and violently destroy his masterpiece

and so he went

leaking insecurities into the minds of other people too

you are not ugly

such nasty words

to describe another human

"ugly freak" he calls her

your "one second word"

built up years of insecurities

it shattered the lens that she saw herself with

you are not ugly

to look a little girl in her eyes

and point out her flaws

beyond her control

is something that i will never understand

saniya kaushal

she told me i should stop eating sugar

he asked why my forehead had so many bug bites

she told me that my skin was wrecked

all unwanted opinions

about the acne on my face

that i already hated myself

you are not ugly

my heart cries for the younger me
the one who was scared to speak up
in fear of drawing attention
to her "ugly" face

saniya kaushal

imagine believing

that people were doing you a favour

by speaking to you

by being seen with you

because society had forced you

to believe

that you were so inferior

you are not ugly

a product of our circumstances

we fight so hard

to believe we are beautiful

saniya kaushal

taken

edited

examined

posted

she desperately waited

for likes and comments

to convince her

she is beautiful

you are not ugly

your words
caused wounds so deep
i thought i'd been shot

saniya kaushal

the words didn't come out your mouth

but you stood there

silently

as i got torn to pieces

so in my mind

your actions

were just as cruel

you are not ugly

he treaded cautiously

being stalked by shadows of self-doubt

inferiority laced his mind

comparing himself to others

he often wondered

why me?

why am i so disgusting?

he was described as

handsome

athletic

smart

funny

kind

brave

passionate

determined

and

ugly

among the beautiful array of words he'd been gifted

"ugly" stood out the most

so much that

he just disregarded the others

you are not ugly

so susceptible to the thoughts of strangers

he wrote off family and friends

as just being biased

each born with a clean slate

a pure heart

self-love

self-confidence

kindness for others

until circumstances change us

in our control

out of our control

events taint our hearts

and people chip away

until eventually those pure hearts become broken

you are not ugly

he internalized his suffering

into darts

he shot recklessly

and ruthlessly

trying to share the pain

and self-hatred

with others

sculpted to believe

that her face

body

sexuality

and ethnicity

served as a stench

repulsive to humanity

withholding them

from even trying to get to know

what laid inside her mind

you are not ugly

reluctant to accept
a single kind word
yet he held on so tightly

sorry for the labels you've been called

sorry for the views that they broke

sorry for the people who called you "too sensitive"

or accused you of "overreacting"

you are not ugly

i'd rather take them too seriously now
than regret not taking them seriously enough later

suicide kills more teens than cancer

so don't tell me

mental health matters less

you are not ugly

you don't know how badly
he wishes you were right
when you tell him
it's all in his head

a looped recording inside my mind

my thoughts never sleep

even when i do

you are not ugly

raised to keep his head down
and hide indoors
while his friends played out
because his mama knew
in the country that they lived in
his beautiful skin
rich in melatonin
was an automatic death sentence
that had stolen the sons
of so many grieving mothers

the self-doubt

seeped into her mind

it brainwashed her

into not chasing the goals

she had dreamed of

her whole life

you are not ugly

i will always stop people
from using labels
because they don't know the deep damage that it causes
but i do

listen...

you are not ugly

are you humble enough

to listen openly

and to accept

you may learn something?

the common sense that everyone knows

but is incapable of following

you are not ugly

to stop the spread

we must fix the root

so teach your children

your little siblings

the younger generations

that making people feel little

should not make them feel big

you think you're being funny by picking on her
you're making your friends laugh, right?
do you also think it's funny how she goes home
and cries?
how she craves the face of someone else?
and feels inferior to everyone around her?

you must think you're a goddamn comedian

you are not ugly

"just joking"

is no longer a get out of jail for free card

saniya kaushal

your definition of beauty

may be different from mine

this does not mean i'm wrong

you are not ugly

shame on you

for believing your opinion was superior to mine

and shame on me

for believing it too

she knows she has pimples

he knows his teeth are crooked

she knows she is a bit overweight

and he knows he's a bit under

it's not your job to point it out

it's not your job to cloud someone's view

of their own beauty

you are not ugly

how about we stop

pointing out features in other people

that they can already see

when they look in the mirror

saniya kaushal

the weight of your words

the severity of their consequences

travel deep & far

so please pick them carefully

you are not ugly

you're accomplished

strong

passionate

and beautiful

but that does not warrant arrogance

make you superior

or give you the right

to put people down

not evil

just careless

careless with her words

because she does not realize the distances they travel

and the depths they reach

you are not ugly

big hearted > big headed

saniya kaushal

do better

you are not ugly

hand on heart
will you look back
and truthfully feel proud
of the way you treated others
and yourself?

saniya kaushal

"but i only said it once"

well "once" is enough
to drop the straw
that finally breaks
the camel's back

you are not ugly

those vile words
you used to describe her

what if they were said
to your little sister?

would your mother be proud
of the derogatory comments
that come carelessly pouring
out of your mouth?

you are not ugly

the first cruel thing that you've said
isn't the first cruel thing that they've heard

so do you really wanna be
their breaking point?

with desperate curiosity

and pain in my heart

i beg of you to answer

what part of pushing them down

builds you up

brings you joy?

you are not ugly

the hurt

the suffering

the tears

you have lived

do not certify you

to spread that pain

to others

you cannot build yourself up

using pieces

you have gathered

from tearing others down

it will not work

you are not ugly

would you feel at ease

raising children

in a world

where people like you

exist?

a chain reaction

of contagious insecurities

spreading from one unsatisfied person to another

a good chunk of humanity

left wishing they were someone else

is that the world

we wish to live in?

you are not ugly

humanity will peak
when bitterness sinks

criticize with intent

directly

don't generalize one mistake

into an entire personality

you are not ugly

save him from the thought

that he's a lost cause

understand the definition

of every word which you use

so their consequences are no longer surprising

you are not ugly

predict the severity your words will cause

and duration they will last

saniya kaushal

just a few short seconds
to type something mean

just a few short seconds
to forget it

but those few short seconds
can cause pain lasting years

you are not ugly

you hit "comment"
on your well-crafted
demeaning remark
towards a stranger
on social media
with the intent
to bring them down

now honestly
what good did that bring you?

a glimpse into his life

through pictures on his feed

but those pictures

don't share his struggles

his broken family

his buried friends

his bedridden days

so choose your words carefully

before you pick out the names

to cowardly call a boy

who you've never even faced

you are not ugly

because it takes the same amount of time

to compliment or to criticize

yet the impact is worlds apart

a single compliment

can save precious hearts

on the verge of shattering

you are not ugly

i don't wanna be a reason
why someone hates themselves
do you?

save your breath

for someone who asks

you are not ugly

a smile on someone's face

or a tear on someone's cheek

you can make the choice

on which you wanna give

saniya kaushal

select your words carefully now

to save yourself

from scrubbing a dirty conscience later

you are not ugly

like a private investigator on the hunt
i search for logic
on why her t-shirt size
is of relevance to you

a high gpa

does not grant you

the intelligence

to deem others as dumb

rather you should realize

the hypocrisy in calling someone dumb

when you barely even know them at all

you are not ugly

deflate
your head

inflate
your heart

saniya kaushal

don't assume you know everything about them
based on the colour of their skin

you are not ugly

stop making fun of a culture
you know nothing about

everyone has opinions

and the ability to control which ones come out

you are not ugly

the worst that will happen if you keep that opinion inside

costs less

than the worst thing that will happen if you let it out

saniya kaushal

born with pure hearts

and big open minds

everyday

we decide

with the choices we make

to keep purifying or start polluting

to keep opening or start narrowing

you are not ugly

if the facial hair
lives on her face

if the large tattoo
travels down his arm

if the cropped shirt
resides on her back

if the piercing
belongs on his eyebrow

and if the neon hair
comes out of her head

why is it so bothersome to you?

they don't want your pity

they want your understanding

you are not ugly

i bet if it was you

who avoided the grocery store

in fear of touching baskets

touched by countless others

i bet if it was you

who spent every morning praying

you wouldn't suffer through another panic attack

i bet if it was you

who woke up everyday

feeling like a burden

i bet if it was you

fighting with your mind

you would never question the reality

of mental health again

nerves before a driver's test

is not clinical anxiety

an independent sad thought

is not clinical depression

washing your hands before a meal

is not obsessive-compulsive disorder

so don't underestimate

what they are actually going through

you are not ugly

keep in mind that you are not there

when she cries herself to sleep

when she curses at herself

when she yells at her reflection

when she misses her medication

so you are nobody to tell her that she's making it up for

attention

saniya kaushal

underestimating the severity of mental health
is throwing future generations
in the way of oncoming traffic

you are not ugly

ask the mourning mother

the lonely little brother

or the heartbroken friends

of the boy who took his life

next time you challenge the credibility of mental illness

saniya kaushal

control the connotations

your words carry

you are not ugly

1) stop spreading hate
2) start spreading love

overcome...

you are not ugly

i know you've been chipped at
i know you've been labelled

i hope to empower you enough
to relabel yourself

the love this world can offer you

heavily

outweighs the hate

you are not ugly

the biggest sin of all
would be letting their words
build a home in your head

how do we let a whole life of self-love

get shattered by a few moments of hate?

i know it is hard

but we can do better

you are not ugly

don't go falling in love with other people

until you have fallen in love with yourself

saniya kaushal

be picky

with the people who you allow into your life

select people

who will neither sugarcoat

nor slaughter you

you are not ugly

engraved in your head

scarred in your heart

don't let those ugly names

define who you are

protect yourself from cruelty

seeping into your head

don't let them change

how you feel about yourself

you are not ugly

in regard to feeling holes in your beauty

i encourage you to check

the credibility of your sources

you know better than to believe them

you know better than to entertain them

because you know damn well

that just because they said that

it does not make it true

you are not ugly

they may not stop

but you can start

to set yourself free

from the pressure to please

anyone but yourself

vulnerability is the bravery

to reflect on burning pain

and relive deep suffering

for the growth of others

and oneself

you are not ugly

use your pain

as a tool

to educate others

if everyone had identical

talents

passions

faces

features

and bodies

our world would be one dimensional

you are not ugly

dye your hair or don't

put make-up on or don't

get a tattoo or don't

grow a beard or don't

get a piercing or don't

shave your legs or don't

do what you wanna do

not what you think you should

according to society's list of do's and don'ts

take control

of what you can

of yourself

and the way

you analyze words

and let them impact you

you are not ugly

don't rely on it stopping

because reality is that it won't

there are always people

middle school

high school

university

workplaces

social media

who will disapprove of you

so what can you stop?

the effect it has on you

saniya kaushal

feel empowered

by your ability

to remain unstoppable

despite harsh speed bumps

challenging roadblocks

and unexpected dead ends

you are not ugly

she is strong

she is smart

she is caring

she is resilient

she is determined

she is passionate

she is beautiful

he is strong

he is smart

he is caring

he is resilient

he is determined

he is passionate

he is beautiful

you are not ugly

i dare you to choose kindness even though you've been given hate

saniya kaushal

don't make choices

about yourself

in hesitation

and fear

of how you will justify yourself

because the only person

who deserves an explanation

is you

you are not ugly

a chain reaction

of contagious compliments

spreading from one self-fulfilled person to another

a once contagious hate

transforms into love

a good chunk of humanity left loving themselves

this is the world

i wish to live in

dig out the seed

so insecurities don't grow

replace it with a flower

that blooms with self-love

you are not ugly

because self-love does not equate to self-completion
and self-confidence does not equate to narcissism
so never feel guilty for loving yourself
but never stop growing either

remove the conditions
on the love
you feed to yourself

you will prosper more
than ever before

you are not ugly

because baby, you are ever-changing

and one day

i hope you grow

into your body

and into your mind

to admire yourself

the way i do

you are not ugly

love from friends is a gift

love from family is a treasure

love from yourself is a set of wings

allowing you to soar

over obstacles

and into blue skies

saniya kaushal

those words became the glue

which molded her

stronger and kinder

than ever before

you are not ugly

the strength you have shown
is the mental equivalence
of moving mountains
or fighting dragons
with your bare hands

don't let the magic of your architecture be broken

for you were built strong enough

to withstand tornados

earthquakes

hurricanes

and tsunamis

you are not ugly

growth does not stop
once confidence is reached

resist the pressure to succumb

to the fabrications of beauty

set by society

you are not ugly

there's more than one definition of beautiful

in fact

there's over seven and a half billion

your body works too hard

physically and emotionally

for you to believe a single negative word about yourself

especially from a stranger

you are not ugly

don't conform yourself
into the labels
they have given you

don't let a day

tarnish

a lifetime

you are not ugly

save others

from the pain

you suffered through yourself

allow yourself

to recognize

the unstoppable person that you are

you are not ugly

a flawed action
does not make you
a flawed person

aware of your actions

accept

an ugly mistake

does not make you an ugly person

and you are capable of better

moving forward

you are not ugly

maybe

a lover

or a friend

or a peer

maybe

a relative

or a colleague

or a stranger

it doesn't matter who said it

it doesn't mean they were right

saniya kaushal

brick by brick
break down the walls
blocking your ability to accept yourself

brick by brick
break down the walls
blocking your ability to love yourself

brick by brick
build yourself up
bold enough to finally be
unapologetically yourself

you are not ugly

young

middle-aged

or old

female

male

transgender

gender-fluid

or other

straight

gay

lesbian

bisexual

or other

african

caucasian

indian

or other

let this be a reminder that it is our differences and
individuality that make us beautiful

you are more than enough

and don't let them convince you otherwise

you are not ugly

labels are dangerous
to ourselves and to others

labels are cruel
quick to come out
but deep enough to cause lasting pain

labels crush confidence
raised to see herself as beautiful
now disgusted by her own reflection

labels are careless
he doesn't even remember calling her names
yet the scar on her heart is deep

saniya kaushal

labels are derogatory
freak, idiot, failure, slut, fat
ugly, skinny, boring, twat

but
people are strong
strong enough to know that the reckless words of others
do not define us

and people are resilient
enough to empower ourselves in a way
so that labels can no longer break us

you are not ugly

smile at yourself
often

they should know better
than to put others down
yet they choose not to

so you should know better
than to believe them

you are not ugly

empower yourself

by breaking down cruelty

before it breaks you

and now

i simply do not care

if they think i am ugly

because i have built myself to know

that my opinion of myself

is what matters the most

you are not ugly

don't spend your time chasing

a reality

that they want

but you don't

they will always

always

always

always

find something to change in you

so achieve satisfaction within yourself

you are not ugly

i need you to know
that the opinion of a few
is not an accurate depiction
of who you really are

how liberating would it feel

to know that you are beautiful

even when people try to tear you down

to know that you are enough

even when people try to point out your flaws

and to feel content with your identity

even knowing that some people are not

you are not ugly

seven and a half billion people

with seven and a half billion opinions

so don't let the thoughts of a dozen people

allow you to question yourself

your beauty is not defined

by the opinions of others

inside or out

read it again

you are not ugly

now look at your reflection

with confidence and a smile

and remind yourself

that you are not ugly

just because they said that you are

when they try to make you feel smaller

come back taller

standing stronger

and feeling prouder

of who you are

you are not ugly

the sum of your values

actions

and ability for reflection

is what defines you

not their whispers

or ignorant judgements

but since an opinion isn't built off of facts

i'll kindly let it go

you are not ugly

don't convince yourself that no one cares

because if it's not your parents

siblings

friends

or classmates

it's the girl on the anonymous helpline

who went through days of training

so she could help save precious lives

just like yours

stop hiding yourself

you have nothing to be ashamed of

you are not ugly

share your burdening thoughts

you no longer have to
suffer alone in silence

you are not ugly

i impatiently wait for the day
where people can finally live freely
without their self-worth being vacuumed out
with the force of a blaring tornado

nothing is more vindicating

than coming back stronger

and looking straight into his eyes

while standing taller

unwavering

with confidence

you are not ugly

self-satisfaction

to a point

where opinions of others

don't sway your self-worth

rise outwards

from the walls of hatred

that others and yourself

have built around you

until you are no longer trapped

you are not ugly

it really pinched his ego

once he realized

nothing he could say

would shatter the faith

i had relentlessly built in myself

i untied my arms

from the heavy ropes

your words constricted me with

i kicked off the padlocks

from the painful chains

your judgements battered me with

i ripped off the mask

from my suffocated eyes

that your humiliation blinded me with

and now i'm free to see myself for who i am

instead of what you tried to make me believe

you are not ugly

taken

edited

examined

and posted

she smiled

because she was happy

and free from a hunt

to find self-worth

saniya kaushal

not a victim

but a warrior

who has channeled pain

into strength

to empower others

and herself

you are not ugly

the kindness of your heart

overflows

it trespasses

into the minds of people

who are not kind to themselves

every time someone called me incapable

it added pressure to my acceleration

and now

i am soaring

you are not ugly

if i hadn't loved myself so little then
i wouldn't love myself so much now

thank you

my heart poured out

and you embraced it

so with immense gratitude

i thank you

for taking the time

to explore life

through my lens

moving forward

please remember

you are not ugly

you are beautiful

i know you are beautiful

because we are all beautiful

every single one of us

in our own

perfectly imperfect way

About the Author

Saniya Kaushal is a daughter, sister, friend, student, poet, and now author of her first book *you are not ugly*. She has always dreamed of sharing her heart with the world through writing. Her own experiences growing up, coupled with heartbreak from watching people shatter one another with their words, were the inspiration behind this collection of poetry. Born in England and raised in Canada, Saniya is soon beginning medical school in Ireland. She adores her family and friends, enjoys baking, watching movies, and of course, writing. You can visit her website at www.saniyakaushal.com.

Manufactured by Amazon.ca
Bolton, ON